So Good

a poet's pen

Felicia Sherelle

POWER PRESS

So Good
A Poet's Pen

by Felicia Sherelle

ISBN 979-8-9935641-0-4

This is a work of poetry. Names, characters, businesses, places, events, locales, and incidents are either the products of the author's imagination or used in a creative, respectful manner. Any resemblance to actual persons, living or dead, or actual events is purely coincidental or used with permission.

Original front cover photograph by Taylor Capers
Back cover photograph and interior background
photograph by Ameerah Shabazz
Cover design and book layout by Maggie Pagratis

Published by Power Press
2025

For my firstborn, who pushed this project.

You are forever my beautiful baby girl,

and forever my friend.

Contents

Soooooo Good

♪ It's so good

Loving somebody

When somebody loves you back

That's a fact

It's so good

Wanting somebody

When somebody wants you back ♪

For you.

my love

runs deep.

Deep like waves of inner peace

And peace....

like that river

I marvel at my superhero

I can think of no other place

That sits well enough with my soul

That fits tight enough around my-OH!

God killed it when he made you

He sho nuff broke the mold

Cuz I'm myself around you

In the same hood

I grew up around you

Vulnerable around you

Safe and secure around you

You make me put all the guns away

With you I'm just a 'round the way girl

Living a 'round the way dream

With my 'round the way king

Your intellect

To die for

Your imagination

I live for it

Your humility

I'm here for it

I never loved a black man in a beard until I met you

You're my bearded warrior

My Swahili conqueror

A Mandinka chief counselor

Both Malcolm and Martin inside you

Words of wisdom for all the homies around you

Cuz they too

Look up to you

When you out here showing 'em opportunity

Training up men

And building up community

Preaching on unity

And doubling down with the brothers on purity

You still make it home in time to grease my scalp

And I'm inspired by your wisdom

When we open the book

and we building about Daniel

Then you teaching on Samuel

And your insight as a black man you…

You…

You just make me in awe of EVERY way how you
handle...

...God's true love

Cuz you are the embodiment of His grace

And I'm just blessed to be part of your journey

So when I'm stroking your beard

I'm really praying a covering over you!

I'm not concerned about losing my sensibility

Cuz I trust you with the inner me

Never a question about loyalty

You consistently speaking into me

After all these years

I'm so secure in how you handle me

My secret keeper

You've been a best friend to me

Even when I lose my wits about me

Of everything you could offer her

You don't rough talk this delicate flower

But you water her

And that's who you are

And that's who you've been

My confidant

Love in another dimension

You see him, that's me

I'm his extension

Pushing me to be better

Holding me up as queen

Without making yourself any lesser

Even my toes get your affection

I'll love you even if you don't put the toilet seat down

Cuz you been down for me

And I'm gon' be down for you

And we ten toes down together

And life is hard enough

But stick with it if you got it like us!

My love,

I could never pay you for what you're worth

so consider this a deposit!

or just the gratuity!

For all the security

And the ingenuity

For making us a priority

With so much sincerity

An example for all to see

And for the patience...

And the kindness...

And the leadership...

And the laughter...

And the love that you bring me

Cuz it's so good

Loving somebody

When somebody loves you back

It's so good

Wanting somebody

When somebody wants you back

Dancing to Death

*As appears in *Brownstone Poets 2024 Anthology*
Nominated for a Pushcart Award, 2024

Dancing to death with ricocheting rockets on the rise

And heaping helpings of hissing hot hints of horror

Downstream are dollops of debris atop decaying dead

With a scent of savagery soot

And a fume of fermented. fiery. flesh.

Seeing smoke afar

And simultaneously

The sight of a slithering snake settling on the side of a
sunken silhouette

Of a masked man.

Who managed to make it more minutes beyond the
mark of madness

Then found himself mashed in the middle of this
makeshift massacre.

He passed.

But not before more atrocities amassed

across an abyss of ash

And add. To that - a tortuous task

Sifting through soil

Sadly

In search for shells of stained sickly souls

Hush!

While we hope to hear a heart's hum

Or a mouth's mumble

Not a growl

Nor a grumble

Not a gasp

But we got a grenade!

And a meticulously misused missile

Oh my!

They leveled the local liveliness

Lethally

They victimized the villagers

Pillaged the parishioners

Killed the kids

Snuffed out the soldiers

And wiped out witnesses

Battling brothers

Bickering brutes

Ishmael. Issac.

With their last breath.

Danced.

To their deaths.

Poets are Prophets

Many are called. Few are chosen.

But poets are prophets

When your spirit's held hostage

It's a poet!

That sets you free.

Ill mics.

Achoo!

Hai-kus.

Bless you.

Ping pong POW!

Poem hittas

Alliteration

Word inspirations

For generations

Like verbal volcanos

And vowels

It's in the voice

It's in the vernacular

And voila!

It's a vibe

Poets tell the mysteries

the secrets

the stories

Expose all the lies

Written in history

And the same lies told repeatedly

Like in the 60s.

When a poet told you ain't no wayyyy...

they shot a president's head clean off in broad day.

And didn't nobody know nothing about it.

Oswald ain't do it!

See

A poet just told you that.

Poets are prophets

We are

declarers of the good news

Poets are prophets

Even bearers of the blues

Poets are teachers

Poets are preachers

Poets are historians

Poets are journalists

Biographers

Poets are storytellers

Story readers

Story interpreters

You knew why Sean Bell had a widow before he even
got married

Because of a poet

You knew that a pack of cigarettes could kill but selling
a loosey was lethal in New York

Because of a poet

Because of a poet you know Da Nile is a river in Africa

Administrative leave with pay is vacation.

I feared for my life is code.

Stop resisting is code.

Obey my commands is code.

I rebuke you in the name of Jesus.

That's not code.

She called that like she saw it.

See.

a poet just said all that.

A poet explained that ain't no mountain high enough

Then a poet told you to put some respect on her name

A poet asked you what's love got to do with it.

A poet sang out BROTHER! BROTHER!

there's far too many of you dying.

You knew why the caged bird sung

You knew that somebody blew up America

You knew Langston Hughes

James Baldwin. Little Ms. Amanda.

Maya feels like auntie.

And Nikki G.

Feels like y'all could have coffee.

Because of a poet

Poets squeeze sweet from bitter

Or expose the real bitter behind the sweet

Because really

Poets are prophets

It's 66 books of poetry out there with the greatest love
story ever told

A poet commanded dry bones to live

A poet told you God got plans to prosper you

A poet anointed a little teenager as king

A mother gave birth to a poet.

After she carried on so hard in prayer that they said she was drunk.

A poet told you in the psalms clear as day who was his Shepherd.

A poet told you stay humble

Then he took a beating for you

Died on a tree

And said anything is possible in Him if you believe

That poet rose in 3 days

This poet says in Him she puts her faith.

A poet taught you about Pettus Bridge

About Danziger Bridge

And how they shot those boys up during Katrina

About Ruby Bridges

A poet's been your bridge over troubled waters!

A poet told you that Trump lost...twice

A poet asks: remember that time Russia helped him out?

A poet told you Harriet stayed strapped

So why were you shocked about Malcolm?

Chairman Fred needed a strap too

Cuz it really be your own people.

And who told you to call it the rebellions not a riot

Call it mass suicide

Not a epidemic

Call it genocide

Not brutality

Not food deserts

Not broken education

Not mass incarceration

It's called pick a ninja off.

One by one.

Who told you all that?

A poet!

That's who!

Cuz poets are prophets

Poets are truth tellers

Proverbial word slayers

Poets asked where were the weapons of mass
destruction

Poets are still waiting.

Poets tell you the truth about the fake beef with Iran.

We shipped them weapons for 16 years.

We broke from England

But God save the king

My country tis of thee

Same melody

A poet just told you that.

And who won't let you forget that Fidel was just
minding his own business?

Just like the Native Americans

And who

And who

And who

And who make sure you never forget?

Hitler was once Time Magazine Man of the Year

Poets.

We do that

Cuz poets are prophets.

I Belong at the Ritz

With its fancy curtains and keyless entry

I belong there

So do you

and you

and especially you.

We belong at the Ritz

Crisp clean white sheets

Not with face holes cut out

But unbothered

Creaseless

Divine even

I like my sheets without holes in them

The Ritz Carlton!

The brochure says

The gold standard for luxury experiences

An unwavering commitment to service

The police say they serve too

So when I walk by the Ritz

they ask me if I'm lost

But I belong there!

I belong here!

On this stolen land

Not more than the Lenape people!

This land is their land.

From California to the New York island

They!

Belong.

at the Ritz for real

With its fancy

ho-tel smell

As if the hoods and ghettos of America don't have a
fancy story of their own to tell

with their potholed streets

Stripped bare of dignity

by underfunding the arts

And overpaying police

While criticizing the educators

Politicians sucked dry of integrity

Devilish corporate greed.

Using Covid to justify inflated dreams

Tax breaks for outsiders to overdevelop by any means

Raised the rents to heights unseen.

The caucasity of these travesties

But as for me.

I belong at the Ritz

With my click clack clogs

And breathtaking beach breeze

But the doorman keeps staring at me

He wonders if I'm in the place I should be

I tell him I am.

This is my hotel

My people are free!

I have a room key

and everything.

Sometimes you gotta stand against the giant you see

Or be relegated to inferiority

Then subjugated as the enemy

But it's the Ritz Carlton baby!

Not mama's baby

Sickly. swaddled.

between the slacks of the shack out back

While the white baby suckled magic gold dust from her
rack.

No, not mama's baby

But it's the Ritz

My baby

And I belong here

With all its splendor.

And mine.

And all its history.

And mine.

And all its amenities.

I have quality extras too!

Like the fact that I come from a long line of ancestry

From people who made it 'cross the Biiiiiig river

Who survived the trip

They didn't jump over

Didn't get thrown over

But made it alive to these shores

And I don't know where exactly they came from

But today

I get to tell their stories

at the Ritz

How they survived.

How they didn't die.

And how they built this damn hotel.

How they made it possible for Mr. Ritz or Mrs. Carlton

or whomever

To have 5 different flavors of soap to offer me

I belong at the Ritz

Even if it's to tell this story

I belong at the Ritz

Where the pool is always open

The exercise machines are always clean

Pinky finger danishes

Washed down with rich, smooth coffee

For free.

Or maybe not.

After forced labor was suspended permanently

People that looked like me

finally got a chance to chase the American dream

While the Ritz and the Carlton families

already had the jump on generational wealth before me.

And before my ancestry

That were born before me

That came to this land before me

And before every other person whose sweat built wealth
for this country.

So now when I stroll up to the Ritz

And the doorman opens the door for me

I walk in like I belong there

Like I built the place

Like I cultivated the land underneath.

I yell down the hall just to hear my echo

But instead I hear my ancestry

Who forced cooked recipes

Even though they first-cooked them in a faraway land.

And before that

got those recipes from their ancestry

In that same far away land

And now they're being cooked in the kitchen at the
Ritz.

Some salt.

A lil pepper

A dash of dignity

A pint of pride

Mixed Martin in a pot of panthers.

Then turned the heat up to hell naw.

Like my ancestors wouldn't set the city on fire for me to
have all the things ever took from them.

And quite literally

to have everything

their sweat built for me

In this grand ole country.

I ignore the lady walking out the hotel with the poodle
in her arms

and with a chauffeur driver not far behind.

She doesn't look my way in the lobby.

Her nose is stuck in the air.

And she's not aging gracefully like me anyway

So...

I don't really care

I place my card onto the desk.

I say, "My room please."

It takes a bit to find me

So I have time to look around

The paint

The marble

The architecture

The annoyed family of 5 waiting behind me

They don't look like me

Maybe they're in a hurry

Maybe they've traveled 500 miles to catch up to me

Maybe they're tired

Because every time they turn on the TV

Another heist of their culture

Another blow to their progress

Another dismissal of their history

Another bullet to their humanity

And a bunch of self-inflicted injuries

No need for me to stare too long at them

Cuz remember

I was building the Ritz!

While they were building for their heirs

And I

belong at the Ritz

My money is green

Just. like. theirs

The Blues

Broken blue crayons

Broken blue pens

Broken blue markers

They all do the same.

So I never knew why depression is called the blues.

I prefer blue ink

I loved the pretty blue dress I wore for 8th grade graduation

I got a pair of blue Manolo Blahnik 4-inch heels wrapped in plastic in the back of my closet

I'm New York blue all day

Go Giants!

My dog is a blue nose

My grandmother fed me blueberries when my mama wasn't looking.

My daughter's first piece of art was in blue crayon

Blue.Blue.Blue

Royal blue!

Looks amaaaaazing on me in the light

My daddy said his first Chevy was blue

I lived in a blue house when I first met my husband

I love my sapphire jewels.

A bluejay visits my porch in the mornings

My first goldfish was blue

My diamond shines blue in the sun so I'm sure that it's
real

I wrapped my baby in a blue blanket when he came
home from the hospital

Blue lights cure my U.V. nails

Jet Blue has the best rates

I

love

blue

So why is depression called the blues?

Is it 400 years of trauma

and when we got a taste of freedom

Here come

Jim Crow

in

white sheets

Sitting at

Pennsylvania Avenue

Plotting with the boys in blue

Burning crosses with orange flames too

What blasphemy!

And in the high court

We had the black robes

send

Dred Scott home

but

that was never his home - know your place

And the songs we penned to paper at the time

Looking for an escape from these traumas inside

And we drank a bit

Ok.

We drank alotta bit

And our instruments played tunes

And we named it the blues

But they stole that too

Or maybe it's the ocean, right?

Its hue

Its blue

But its waves crash

Digging up cemeteries of my ancestors past

The blues comes from the blue devil.

Meaning to drink in excess

Not the other evil

You know the one

Keep a few

Sell off the rest

Dividing families. Cultures. Storytelling and philosophies.

Enslavement led to generations of ill mentalities

But what about the blue paint that chipped the wall in the projects

Or. The.

white man's blue veins prepped for the poison

Or. A.

man's blue suede shoes that paced outside of a little girl's bedroom door

Or. The.

blue handled baseball bat a boy saw his daddy swing at his mama's head

Or. A.

doctor's blue covered footwear walking to the waiting room to announce he's killed her

She's finally dead

It was the color of the screen when the cable was out.

It was also a blue note my daddy owed to a loan shark that took him out.

The blues. The blues. The blues.

The blues I can't escape

The blues that taps my shoulder and announces itself

It's never late

It rents space in my head for free

And when I think I've escaped it

Here it comes

Dark blue clouds chasing after me

And then comes its cousin...CAN'T SLEEP

Its parents...RELIVE PAST TRAUMA

Its daughter...SUICIDAL THOUGHTS

Its son...EMOTIONAL DRAMA

Its nieces. Its nephews...IRRITATION and
AGITATION

And its most prized possessions

Financial hardships and poor relationships

I.cry.out to it

We fight.

Me and the blues.

We battle

Depression get OFF me!

Literally sick in your company!

You show up to destroy me

Sent to crush me and annoy me

disguised as my favorite color

Too familiar like my mother or my brother

But maybe blue ain't it

Maybe I need another

Cuz

I

Was

Never

Meant

To Be....

Broken. blue. crayons.

Broken. blue. pens

Broken. blue. markers

But what's your favorite color?

Universal Nurturers

*As appears in *Whisper, Whisper, Shout* (2025)

Me.

The consuming fire that sashays through the galaxy

Moon dust trapped between my toes

Meets him

The burning ember that ignites the whole Milky Way

And together

We own this forest!

Or will burn it down trying

I stand nearly seven light years tall.

I sip tea with God.

My legs dangle from heaven and rest somewhere in the Amazon.

I.

Am.

Glorious.

He.

Poaches himself atop Saturn's rings

He directs meteor traffic

And stretches his arms through constellations just to
caress my face

He's so playful

But.

He.

Is.

Colossal.

In the afternoons, I listen for the deepness in his voice
when he roars

Thunder.

When he misses me

Rain.

When he huffs. Childishly bidding me closer

Wind.

And when we finally embrace

Taste the rainbow!

We.

Are.

Climactic.

In the mornings, we chase the sun for fun

He helps me onto an asteroid

I ride high past Mercury

During our evening walk

We toss the moon into its place

Sometimes we knock down satellites

And rock Pluto to sleep

When I'm in the saltiest of moods

Fire and brimstone

They blast from my ears

When he needs a smile

I pluck the tip of Mount Everest and blow snow in his face

We are the UNIVERSE-SOUL nurturers

Space is our playground

We are larger than life

Our mood commands cosmic activities

A cough and a head cold

Sends hoards of geese flying home

We have a fallout over Mars

Across the sky that night

They'll be no stars

But a solar eclipse when we make up with a kiss

It's his birthday on 4th of July

And there's a laser show in our skies

The fastest moving comets are the result of tussling in
our very own space garden

Balance is our desire

But conflict is in our nature

Sometimes a galactic catastrophe

Other times a celestial star baby

I Was Born this Way

I was born this way

With this black skin

The mother of civilization

With these wide hips

And these plush lips

And somewhere down the line

this white man's complexion

I was born.

This way.

In this pain wrought skin

Pain in my back

Pain in my heart

Pain in my walk

Pain in my talk

Pain in my soul

Pain in the neck

Pain over and over again

I was born this way.

I was born with these hands

I was born this way

These hands

These feet

These ways that life can't teach

These hands create and shape anything

Or should I say everything

Into a sudden surprise

I make everything come alive

More than my womb gives life

I'm kissed by the sun

The same sun that chased my ancestors' feet

I was born this way

In a land that don't grieve me nor receive me

Nor my offspring

From my mother's 16-year-old wounds

Born female and black

It's a fact

I was born this way

A whole community rides my back

I make ends meet

All with my creativity

I lower the temperature in a room

Hailed as a hero for all to see

But it's quietly

That I sob silently

This weight

Too great

These brown eyes

Alone and lonely

I bury these cries

I was born this way.

I'm every woman

doing it naturally

Sun up to sundown

I do it like it's 10 of me

The glue that holds the family

And with a divine energy

Daily battle with the enemy

Ten steps ahead of the trickery

I was born this way

Overlooked by society

Accused by Karen

Expected to be superhuman

My body.But your vote tells me what to do with it.

I was born this way.

The oceans and the fields still hold my DNA

And the whips and the chains

I was stolen south bound freight

Since then

I been begging

Please.

Let me be great.

I was born this way.

My survival remains a mystery

You so frustrated by what you can't understand about
me.

So you disrespect me

respectfully

MISunderstood that you really come from me

Without me you'd have no history

Every one of Africa's resources exploited

So pick and choose

But civilization

It came from MY womb

I was born this way!

I'm the motherland's real blood diamond.

I said pick and choose

But we ain't picking cotton!

I was born this way!

My hair commands so much attention

My backside on display

with zero commission

My style imitated

My speech duplicated

Everything about me scrutinized

My community pillaged

then gentrified

While my sons are pulverized

But it's still justified

I was born this way.

To level up

far beyond what you think I'm able

I was born this way

I don't pull up a seat

I carry in the whole damn table

I was born this way

Everything I touch multiplies

I was born this way

I can crush a whole kingdom with my thighs

But I promise

It ain't no magic to this strength inside

It comes down the generations

From women with little education

Who planted seeds of greatness

Who imparted wisdom that inspired nations

They fought wars in streets and homes

We encouraged oppressed men

Our best men

And out of desperation we became the backbones

The ability to rise

After everything life throws

Us women. We might trip a little

But we will never fold!

We are healers of brokenness

Whatever I have

I give generously

Outsiders question my royalty

But I wear this crown permanently!

Even from a dry place

I pour out enough for all of us

And even though I'm mishandled

I

Just

Love

Harder

I was born

this way.

You Steal My Soul

I dreamed about us last night

And I saw you standing

And waiting for me

You motioned me closer and

That knocking thing happened in my knees

When you bit your lip

And I remember what that meant

My heart

My heart it fluttered

and

You didn't even need to say nothing

It was the gaze of your eyes

As if I was the woman you had waited for all your life

As if I was the moon

You

just

gazed at me.

It scared me really

But I was captivated fully

As if I were the deer

And you the hunter

You

Just

Gazed at me

Like I was the missing link

To everything you had ever prayed for

imagined

or could ever think

And my heart

My heart

It fluttered like birds splashing in a pond

It screamed like the Hulk

But it ached at how much time had gone

And my body

My body

You remember how it's captivating like the green rolling hills

It stood erect

Unable to budge

It was glistening and still

And then you cocked your neck to the side

Oh why did u do that?

Just…

Just staring at me

And the little girl inside me blushed

But I turned away so you couldn't see

That was pretty much all to the dream

But it got me to thinking

What's happening to me?

Why am I on you like this?

Why am I tripping?

I recall how our lips would touch

And you would ever so gently

Breathe in deeply

You'd embrace me completely

And you'd passionately kiss me

Then you'd pull back a bit

And suck in the air from my mouth

It happens electrically

And it's almost magically

That you'd take breath from me

And we exchange automatically

But oddly it's refreshing

And it's all the more surprising

That yet I'm still standing

With my heart only beating

But my soul is just pounding

It. Cries. Yes!

And it's resounding

I'm more alive when you take breath from me

You've just doubled my energy

And somehow

this exchange

Has intertwined us naturally

Clearly

Undeniably

We are 2 souls down to 1

Subtraction mathematically

But you also have the potential

To make me forget your credentials

And forget what I'm missing

I forget you are forbidden

Because you are an ex

And I vowed not this way again

Off limits I mean

Regardless of how great this all seems

But one thing I desire

And it'll be so glorious

If I could think a bit more rationally

And find that inner voice in me

That will wake me

and shake me

And then I'd surely change course in all this

This forbidden love

Gotta be lust and immoral

If I went this way with you

I'm talking something abnormal

Yet I crave your embrace

And the spark of your eye

The fire in your kiss

It's exactly how I remember it

What an epic experience

And a sight to behold

But like a thief in the night

It's you again

coming for my soul

You still…

Still…

Still…

You still

Steal my soul

What's Free

We be free like

We be free like...like

Like the cherry on top

And sometimes

Extra whip cream on the side

We free. We free.

I said we free

We be free like emancipation

We be free like a panther's breakfast

We be free like a extra side of gravy

We free. We free. We free.

We be free y'all.

Like the bitter lemon water from the waitress

That's free.

Yeah. That be us.

We free.

We be free like a shoeshine

We be free like the ocean

Those seashells

We free like them

We be free like the sun

Those expensive rays draw up my roots

And I be free

We free. We free. We free

Like.

kindness.

Mama said it don't cost you nothing to be nice

We free like voting

We only needed a whole movement

And a march

And a congressional law

But we be free y'all.

We be free like Harriet

We be free like Fredrick

We be free like Malcolm

We free. We free.

I said we free.

We be free like freedom riders

We be free like free at last

We be free like 4 little Alabama girls

We be free like bombs over Iraq

We be free like black history week is now black history
month

We be free like that syphilis...

In Tuskegee

We be free like that rock.

from the CIA.

But we did pay a TAX on that one

We free. We free. We free.

I said we free like love.

We be free like dem bullets.

We free like the youngest baby

off to Vietnam

We be free

We free like the mob

We free like ghettos

We free like government cheese

We free.

Like.

Water.

From.

hoses.

Like TVs.

From.smashed. glass. windows

during the language of the unheard

In. the. Streets.

We. Be. free.

We free like creativity and patents

And all the firsts

Like brother Baldwin

And Uncle Baraka

And Daddy Hughes

And Mother Angelou

We be free like them.

We be free like the traffic light

Like the peanut

Like potato chips

Like the gas mask

The blood bank

Refrigerated trucks

Automatic elevator doors

The IBM computer monitor

The tissue holder

The clothes dryer

The dustpan

golf tees

The ice cream scooper

The lawnmower

The lawn sprinkler

The modern toilet

and the mop!

The folding chairs at big mama's funeral

And thee…

Michelle and Barack.

We be free like them.

We be free like Ali's confidence

Ain't nobody never paid for that

We be free like him

His butterfly. And his bee

We be free like all of dem

We be free like a truthful education.

We be free like common sense.

We be free like the golden rule.

We be free like 40 acres

And that mule

We be free like dignity and pride.

Even though

It may cost you

your lives

Fire Next Time

He said

it'll be fire next time

He said it'll be fire next time

No WAAAA-TER!

He said it'll be fire

Fire next time

He said fire

He said fire

He said fire

Next time

No mo water

Too much water

No more ark

No more Noah

No more rains

No 40 days

No more water

He said fire

He said fire

He said fire

next time

Calling all houses!

All houses

Blue ones

Red ones

Big ones

Small ones

Tiny ones

All ones

Calling

All

Houses.

To order...

That's big mouths

That's the judgey ones

Fuzzy ones

On the fence ones

Hang out by the gate called beautiful ones

But.

ain't.

trying

To get wet

with his presence ones...

He said fire He said fire He said fire

...next time

The same fire.

The same fire.

same fire saved your soul.

It's the same fire.

Same fire.

Same fire.

It's coming back

Will you already be home?

He said fire

Fire

He said fire

He said fire next time

It's the same fire

Same fire

Fire of the Holy Ghost

The same fire

Same fire

purify you like gold.

It's the same fire

Same fire

Three kids met in the furnace

The same fire

The same fire

Look again and nothing's burning

He said fire

He said fire

He said fire next time

Sound the alarm

Be ready for the fire

Get right before the fire

Live like it's really fire

Real fire

Real fire coming next time

Hold your tongue

Resist evil

Don't get caught up in the fire

In the fire

He said fire next time

Corruption

No self-control

Dishonesty

No integrity

Living selfishly

Don't get tripped up

Don't get caught up

You don't wanna be in that fire

Cuz He said fire

He said fire.

He really said fire.

Next time....

Yesterday

Had that ugly talk yesterday

With my handsome black son yesterday

Couldn't hold off any longer yesterday

My soul

It couldn't rest yesterday

Until I sat him down

And I told him yesterday

You are different from your peers

You can't do what they do

Reach slow when pulled over son

On the wheel

Hands 10 and 2

When out with your friends son

Either today. Tomorrow. Or yesterday

If police hit the lights

Hear these words clearly when I say

Lower your tone

Don't debate and slow your speech rate

Don't look em in the eye

Cuz it's bound to agitate

And don't talk back

Rest assured

They'll retaliate

With hands on their weapons

It's mostly to teach you a lesson

They'll get close up in your face

Son please

Just let em.

I explained their rules of power

To my beautiful black son yesterday.

To them son, you ain't deserving

Of respect

Humanity

Nor dignity.

No protecting

No serving

Your life ain't worth preserving

Son, I know it's a bit unnerving

But with every encounter they've already determined

You ain't worthy of questioning

Guilty until THEY find you innocent

The police

Play

Prosecutor

Judge

and executioner.

Yesterday, I said son, keep your cool to minimize what
they'll do to ya

It's a tactic to make you the aggressor

Breathe wrong son, and he'll become more aggressive

Even if you try that passive aggression

He'll determine your innocence based on how you
express it

So with a gun pointed at your head

Or

after you're slammed against a window

Or

you're pulled from the car

Or

you're threatened with a taser

Or

After backup arrives

Or you're eating skittles. or drinking iced tea. or blasting music.

Or pulled over for speeding.

Or standing in front of a bodega

Or sleeping in bed

Or you're sitting in your own apartment

In your own living room

eating ice cream...

Keep Calm!

It happened in Texas

His name was Jean

They'll describe you as suspicious

And we'll spend years dismissing it

And when you want to pick up the phone to call me

Son

reaching for your phone right then is costly

I told my son yesterday

They will describe you as combative

No body cam tape to match it

By the time you're unresponsive

They'll be screaming you were uncooperative

Baby boy!

Just come home alive to me!

My son.

My handsome. Tall. Honor student. Athletic. Beautiful

Black son

Turned 13 yesterday

So Yes

today son

You have a right to live

And Yes

today son

We reject that police murder is what it is

And Yes

today son

Your life is a gift

And Yes

today son

We are fighting for a real power shift

Yes today

you can truly represent

Yes today son

you can be the president

Yes. today.

Yes. today.

Yes. today.

Stand against police abuse

Yes today.

We say no more Jim Crow justice rules

And yes

today son

I'm always team you

Yes today son

Be great in this life you choose

My son's black life as an option play?

Who son?

What son?

Under what sun?

Not today.

Enslaved, Enlightened, Entombed: Phillis Wheatley, Tragedy of a Scribe

* NEW RELEASE

I sit and I watch

I sit and I smell

I sit and I feel

I feel knots tangled in my belly

It feels like the big blue ocean we set sail for just five days ago has sucked me under

The sea has swallowed me whole

My little itty bitty body

once wrapped in my father's long strong arms

Now stiff and cold

Nne-Nne

She called out to me

She called me away from the big scary ships

She ran down after me

She begged the men to unhand me

But now, my knees knock

My eyes

Vessels of tears

My soul aches

I. am. here.

In the belly of the beast

The sun beat down low on my village that day

How I wish I could reach up now and touch its rays

to save me

Where. are. they. taking. me?

For

I

am

just

a girl.

Now I sit.

I sit and I watch.

In the corner of this big ugly ship

I spy the three men who spit at the captain

They are surely going overboard today

How I wish

Wish I could hold them

Let them smell my dark thick hair

Maybe it be like medicine to them

Before they go splash

But instead

I sit.

And alone

I watch.

Scared

I smell.

And sorrow

I feel.

I look up at the moon spread across the dark night

I won't move my feet

For God only knows what they will do to me

My bronze toes step off the big ship onto a land I have never known

At 7-years-old

What will be my fate in this here Boston?

This is not my home

There is no uwa here

There is no uba here

But I

am

here.

Being poked and prodded

A pale face named Wheatley calls me hither

I can barely understand her talk

Even though Wheatley be not my name

And Phillis not who I be

It's the name of the ship that brought, bought, and
bartered me

I go.

And yet

There is something gentle about her voice

Me, a stranger

Frail

Broken in spirit

Mistress keeps me close.

So close. I learn English!

Even closer

I learn Greek!

Closer still

I learn Latin!

And as if He came down to recite it Himself

I learn Bible.

Soon, I exchange my mistress bedside for the pen

I talk to my pen

It most certainly talks back

It tells me to write of King George

across those same shores

those same seas I came from

It tells me to write of Commander Washington

Who invites me to Cambridge

A full negress now.

Off to meet the future commander in chief

Next

to London

Where Ben Franklin took a liking to me

And then…

The first kidnapped woman from Africa

Chained

I came to Boston

Polished

By America

I publish for the world!

Poems of Various Subjects, Religious and Moral

My life brochure?

Nabbed from the African shores

To famous published poet

From mistress' young protege

To educated

free

wife

and mother of 3.

From all hope lost on that dreadful sea

To all hope found in my faith

I write more

And more

No blood

Only words fill my veins.

I hear rhymes in my head

Not just thoughts

I. own. this. voice.

for once…

And nobody owns me

finally.

But nobody wants to hear my words this second time
strangely.

And at the same time

my husband

we both in debt. destitute.

and desolate

and then comes demise.

The death of not one

but two of mines.

I am a great American tragedy

Perhaps thee greatest one you'll ever hear about or see.

As my third child and I lie dying together

At age 31

I look over my life

Surely I had the odds beat

I set out to make a legacy

To inspire literary giants coming after me

And to achieve what had never been heard of before me

A lil' Negro lady

and a pen that gave her liberty

But at the end of my life

Who will strike a spark to ignite me?

To revive me

To affirm me

To assure me

Once a stolen girl

Now a lost woman in peril

The only way I'll be found

is if you take the torch from me

And carry out my pen's destiny.

Does my pen whisper to you?

Will you do all it commands?

Does my pen bark at you?

Will you submit to its demands?

Phillis' Pen

Phillis' Diary

Her life story

Please dear hearts

Do not delay

Carry out the dream for me

About the Author

Felicia Sherelle is a published author and poet, journalist, workshop leader, and writing consultant. This publication marks a shift in genres. She is the author and publisher of three children's books before this compilation of poems. As a workshop leader, Felicia instructs emerging poets in the craft. As a consultant, Felicia is a manuscript editor, ghostwriter, book project manager, and publishing press. She is immersed in the literary arts scene in New Jersey where she has helped produce the annual Paterson Poetry Festival since 2017. A Pushcart award nominee, Felicia is a teaching artist for youth in Passaic County Community College's Theatre and Poetry Project. She resides in New Jersey with her two adult children.

Services

- ❖ Manuscript Editing
- ❖ Ghostwriting
- ❖ Publishing Services
- ❖ Book Project Management
- ❖ Adult & Youth Writing Workshops
- ❖ Spoken Word Bookings
- ❖ General Consulting for all book projects including children's books

www.njpowerspaces.com

More Books from the Author

Free Special Gift

AS A THANK YOU FOR YOUR PURCHASE, PLEASE ENJOY THIS EXCLUSIVE SPOKEN WORD AUDIO BY FELICIA SHERELLE

THIS ORIGINAL POEM ENTITLED, "SARAH, B. SMITH, OR SIMONE" IS FEATURED IN THE ANTHOLOGY, *JAZZ POETRY,* CURATED BY NZIMA HUTCHINGS

BACKGROUND SOUNDS ARE COURTESY OF JOHN COLTRANE "NAIMA"